I0693534

북한아, 너냐?

North Korea, Is That You?

Tyler Lazarus Stump

Mister. E

Copyright @ 2024 He Who Rebels Against All

All rights reserved. No part of this document may be reproduced in any form by any electronic or mechanical devices, including information storage or retrieval systems WITHOUT permission from the publisher, except by reviewers, who may quote passages in the form of a review.

ISBN

Fonts by Jess Latham. Thank You.

Printed, Distributed and Bound in the United States of America First Printing

SEPTEMBER 2024

Published by He Who Rebels Against All

Oklahoma City, Oklahoma 73106

Hey, Thanks for getting a copy!
IF you like these, check out my other works
XOXO

North Korea, Is That You?

By TYLER LAZARUS STUMP
AKA MISTER. E

As America **FALLS** from within, as most empires usually do, it's important to focus the lens of scrutiny not **ON** it, as I'd likely be expected to do, but on the outside parallels beyond "ROME" and past nations which have declined, met civil strife and painfully ended.

I turn the attention to another state.

North Korea-r.

As this writing IS being written, fat, ugly liberals with bad hair dye jobs and ukraine flags are in Washington D.C. vandalizing the Liberty Bell (Replica) and Writing "FUCK THE USA" all over the monuments and screaming about Freeing Palestine, and whatever other flavor of the month cause they've now adopted.

They should be adopting weight watchers.

But more than the reality of Palestine vs
Israel,
and now the bandwagon of Ukraine, which these same losers couldn't have even found on a map, prior to 2022,

The disgraceful slide into clear decay isn't just at the populace level.

The people are really the surface level (of things) and represent the dysfunction that is growing, spreading and sprouting... much deeper.. below that level.

Am I surprised to see the US populace

turning on itself?
No, Not after the pandemic and everything it entailed.
Not even in a snide way.
These people are stupid and borderline retarded.

It's to be expected, AT this late hour.

It's to be expected, AT this late hour.
The people bringing the nation to it's knees
isn't the true ISSUE< although the coming
blowjob from the state will be >

It's the press.
It's the media.
It's the 24/7, inflammatory style, curated
outrage that drives FURTHER people to act
stupid, shitty and retarded.

The media, as it's always evoked, usually too
broadly and abstractly is a conglomerate of
… not typewriters and TV's.. that's the 1950's.
It's a smartphone filming some shocking act,
broadcast over the world and through every
social media channel.

It's an echo chamber of error.

It's an interconnected rumbling of

information, all designed to generate clicks, web pages getting opened, and Twitter (X) links, and down the ladder of other major sites the stone loudly falls.

The digital age has brought people to being connected, but now toxically connected.

JUST A CONSTANT HATE TRAIN OF STUFF that makes people lose their minds, get riled up, and is designed to ruffle feathers.

And in this birdcage of bad behavior, there is now lots of BIRD SHIT because of these bird brains not ever knowing how to disengage and disconnect from it all.

As we speak, I'm sure at the above mentioned scene of the capitol being defaced, there are people yelling, screaming, fighting, knocking each other out and spitting on the other.

I can't be bothered with any of it, including the pending civil unrest/ possible civil war styled fight that's been brewing for the last 15 years between extreme right and extreme left.

I don't give a shit if these people kill the other.

Let them go at it.

Maybe, after they're all wiped out, common sense can step out of the shadows and build a country that isn't running on pure dysfunction and insanity.

If they want to kill the other, let them

*flips on sunglasses and floats on my

inflatable Zebra pool float*

sips my frozen strawberry margarita that I loaded with cheap tequila

But more than that...
The thing is, I can deal with chaos of a populace going out of control and spiraling,

I can even deal with a rogue government that is overstepping its executive authority.

BIG BROTHER can be reigned in.

Both of those elements of STATE and PEOPLE, can be dealt with.
It is a pain in the ass, but it's not unfixable.

HOWEVER,
that is ON the condition that you have a
working press and information channels
to open discussion and dissent IN.

We no longer have that.

Hence, the Title.

"North Korea, IS that You???"

All of our media is now state controlled.

In a way that the same STATE is running
out of control and running roughshod
over the very people that are fighting each
other, and allowing no room to push
either out of the way.

The American Government controls and is infiltrated deep inside all of the top channels. It doesn't matter which way the political winds shift, they are in the entire weathervane.

The Press, at least for the last seventy years, has always had SOME manner of allegiance to state channels, but increasingly as time and continuous political scandalous and lies went on, the press began covering up for the state, and now the state has penetrated into the "free press" and cum all over it.

The pages of government coverups are all still sticky.

As I've said before, BIG GOVERNMENT plus BIG MEDIA equals BIG TROUBLE.

You can't defer to CNN, FOX, THE NEW YORK TIMES, or any of these outlets and channels because they are going to be pushing state curated and state favoring narratives.

The reporting isn't reporting.
It's opinion, talking heads that talk out of their asses and the worst excuses for

"journalists" that you have EVER seen.

Or read.

It's now Rachel Maddow putting on a thirty minute fake show and Tucker Carlson blabbing with red cheeks.

That's supposed to be the "peak" of journalism.

These people suck.

Ass.

So, not only do the reporters lean in extremes, the news itself is selective about WHAT it will cover.

Anything TOO truthful, dropped.
Anything TOO revealing to some
politician, person, entity, or federal
agency... completely passed over.

It's all got to favor pre-selected and
curated agendas of right and left,
and GOD help you, if you try and expose
both of them and both of their shitty
"sides" for the frauds they REALLY are.

People who don't understand the proliferation of
information and why it's so important to the health
and vitality of a nation/state, will be confused
why journalism "being dead" is so dangerous.
And wicked.

Once journalism dies... lies can run

rampant.

Nothing keeps it in check.

Corruption becomes normalized.

It also becomes parroted back to the people and colored as "not bad."

In essence,

Society goes to shit.

When information channels are corrupted.

Nothing is there to now keep said corruption in check.

Everything becomes a LIE.

Easily.

The state can starting
feeding people lies,
and people will suckle at
the tit of totalitarianism.

If allowed, the state will
not only angle itself for
ultimate power, but it'll
start silencing and
removing (killing) anyone

who tries to speak TRUTH
back to power.

And in consequence,

people become
POWERLESS
to the regime,
government, federal
power that has control of
the entire landscape.

There is no elections,
no press,

no freedom,

There is ONLY whatever
the state allows,
and it's a theatre show of
what they'll call "freedom."

This.
is.
Why.

Losing. The Press.
Is the start of a slide….

that can't be fixed.

And ends up being

FATAL.

An example of this and how corrosive it becomes is:
AS I wrote this, my phone sent an update about Russian + Chinese planes that were spotted operating in Alaskan airspace and diverted.

Is it true? Can you believe what's being said?
Is that a real update?

DID IT EVEN ACTUALLY HAPPEN???

The slippery slope of this is,
once your news channels become
compromised, in the ways THEY now
are,
it can all be fake news.

And this isn't specific to American
News.

Russian News makes up bullshit ALLL

the time.
Chinese news is the same,
and NORTH KOREAN news, whatever
form of it they get, is DEFINITELY built
on absolute nonsense and state-
sponsored HORSESHIT.

but see, once this destructive process
starts of ruining the integrity of your
journalism sources,

NOTHING can be believed.

Nothing that comes out of the state's
mouth or state channels.

It might all be B.S.

And frequently, commonly, once the
state has full control, IN THE WAY it
now DOES (America)

- it is.

**this is no longer America···
hellur···**

hehrow????

Hehrow???
North Korea????

ISA THAT YOU????????

squints my eyes and looks closely

squints more

becomes Kim Jun Un

Oh, Herrow there.
It's me.
Kimmy Jung III.

THE END.

북한아, 너냐?

North Korea, Is That You?

Tyler Lazarus Stump
Mister. E

www.ingramcontent.com/pod-product-compliance
Lightning Source LLC
Chambersburg PA
CBHW081605250726
48653CB00009B/3563